BURMA 2016 HUMAN RIGHTS REPORT

EXECUTIVE SUMMARY

Burma has a quasi-parliamentary system of government in which the national parliament selects the president, and constitutional provisions grant one-quarter of national, regional, and state parliamentary seats to active duty military appointees; all other seats are open to elections. The military also has the authority to appoint the ministers of defense, home affairs, and border affairs and assume power indefinitely over all branches of the government should the president declare a national state of emergency. In November 2015 the country held nationwide parliamentary elections that the public widely accepted as a credible reflection of the will of the people. The then opposition party, the National League for Democracy (NLD), chaired by Aung San Suu Kyi, won 390 of 491 contested seats in the bicameral parliament. Parliament elected NLD member U Htin Kyaw as president in March and created the position of State Counsellor for Aung San Suu Kyi in April, cementing her position as the country's de facto leader.

Civilian authorities did not maintain effective control over the security forces.

In March the NLD government began its five-year governing term and, beginning in April, released hundreds of political prisoners. During the year civil society noted a sharp and significant, but by no means complete, improvement in their rights to freedom of speech and assembly.

The three leading human rights problems in the country were human rights violations in ethnic minority areas affected by conflict, restrictions on freedoms of speech, and abuses against and restrictions on members of the Rohingya population. Authorities failed to protect civilians in conflict zones from killing, gross abuses, and displacement, but took some preliminary steps to address reports of abuses. While authorities returned approximately 20,000 Rohingya and other Muslim households displaced in 2012 communal violence to their locations of origin inside Rakhine State, more than 120,000 remained displaced in camps. An additional estimated 30,000 civilians were displaced due to the government's security operations beginning in October in response to attacks by militants on Border Guard Police posts in Maungdaw, northern Rakhine State.

Other significant human rights problems persisted, including rape and sexual violence; forced labor; politically motivated arrests; widespread corruption; land-related conflict; restrictions on freedom of speech, assembly, and association; and intimidation and occasional arrests of journalists. Conditions in prisons and labor camps also remained harsh. Trafficking in persons, including forced labor of adults and children, continued.

While the government took some limited actions to prosecute or punish officials responsible for abuses, many such actions by government actors and security officials continued with impunity.

Some ethnic armed groups committed human rights abuses, including forced labor of adults and children and recruitment of child soldiers, and failed to protect civilians in conflict zones.

Section 1. Respect for the Integrity of the Person, Including Freedom from:

a. Arbitrary Deprivation of Life and other Unlawful or Politically Motivated Killings

There were several reports that the government or its agents committed arbitrary or unlawful killings unrelated to internal conflict.

On June 20, a government soldier shot and killed Gum Seng Aung in Myitkyina, Kachin State. Media, police and nongovernmental organization (NGO) reports varied greatly as to the details. Allegedly, Gum Seng Aung and another individual were crossing a bridge when another group harassed them. They asked nearby soldiers for assistance, leading to an apparent scuffle that resulted in Gum Seng's death. Reports indicated his body was found more than two miles from the location of the conflict, drawing further questions as to the veracity of the official description of events. Residents carried the body of Gum Seng Aung through the streets of Myitkyina as a martyr. Media reports indicated that the soldiers responsible for Gum Seng Aung's death turned themselves in to local police. Authorities charged the soldiers with manslaughter and turned them over to the military for subsequent investigation. Military officials held a closed tribunal following an investigation. On November 29, they held a public hearing in Myitkyina attended by 16 civil society representatives, including family and friends of the victim. At the hearing a soldier admitted to shooting Gum Seng Aung accidentally. The jury did not reach a verdict or sentence the soldier by the end of the year, agreeing on the need for additional time to deliberate further.

In September the Kachin Baptist Convention submitted a letter to the UN special rapporteur on human rights in Burma asking for assistance in the investigation of the January 2015 deaths of two Kachin volunteer schoolteachers. The teachers, Maran Lu Ra and Tangbau Hkawn Nan Tsin, were found dead in Kaung Hkar Village, Muse District, and Shan State. Civil society and the media claimed members of the Burmese Army 503 Battalion raped and killed the women, while government officials argued that the forensic evidence did not implicate the military or indicate rape. The Baptist group had established an independent inquiry commission in February 2015, but it continued to report insufficient cooperation from the military and police.

Arbitrary and unlawful killings related to internal conflict also occurred (see section 1.g.).

b. Disappearance

There were no reports of politically motivated disappearances of private citizens outside of conflict-affected border states (see section 1.g.).

c. Torture and Other Cruel, Inhuman, or Degrading Treatment or Punishment

While the law prohibits torture, members of security forces reportedly tortured, raped, beat, and otherwise abused prisoners, detainees, and other citizens and stateless persons in incidents not related to armed conflict. Such incidents occurred, for example, in Rakhine and Kachin States.

Security forces reportedly subjected detainees to harsh interrogation techniques designed to intimidate and disorient, including severe beatings and deprivation of food, water, and sleep. Authorities reportedly no longer used burnings and water torture as a common practice, but human rights groups continued to report incidents of torture in conflict-affected states. As in previous years, authorities took little action to investigate incidents or punish alleged perpetrators.

There were credible reports of rapes of women in Rakhine State, including by security forces, that local authorities and security forces failed to investigate or prosecute alleged perpetrators (see sections 1.g. and 1.d.).

Prison and Detention Center Conditions

Conditions in prisons and labor camps continued to be harsh due to overcrowding, degrading treatment, and inadequate access to quality medical care and basic needs, including food, shelter, and hygiene.

<u>Physical Conditions</u>: The Correctional Department operated an estimated 43 prisons and approximately 48 labor camps, officially called "agriculture and livestock breeding career training centers" and "manufacturing centers," according to the government. More than 20,000 inmates were serving their sentences in 46 of these centers across the country, where prisoners could opt to serve a shortened period of their prison sentence in "hard labor," which was considered by many as more desirable.

A human rights group and prominent international NGO estimated there were approximately 60,000 prisoners--50,000 men and 10,000 women--held in separate facilities in prisons and labor camps. Estimates placed the number of juvenile detainees at a few hundred. Overcrowding was reportedly a problem in many prisons and labor camps. Some prisons held pretrial detainees together with convicted prisoners and occasionally held political prisoners together with common criminals.

Medical supplies and bedding were often inadequate. Bedding sometimes consisted of a single mat, wooden platform, or laminated plastic sheet on a concrete floor. Prisoners did not always have access to potable water. In many cases family members supplemented prisoners' official rations with medicine and basic necessities. Inmates reportedly paid wardens for basic necessities, including clean water, prison uniforms, plates, cups, and utensils.

Detainees were unable to access quality and timely medical care. Prisoners suffered from health problems, including malaria, heart disease, high blood pressure, tuberculosis, skin diseases, and stomach problems, resulting from unhygienic conditions and spoiled food. The prevalence of HIV/AIDS and other sexually transmitted infections in prisons reportedly remained high. Former prisoners also complained of poorly maintained physical structures that provided no protection from the elements and had rodent, snake, and mold infestation.

There were reports of custodial deaths due to health problems associated with prison conditions and lack of quality and timely medical care. Between 2011 and 2014, 120 persons reportedly died in 46 of the prisons and labor camps, reportedly from "weather, diet, lifestyle, and accidents."

Prison conditions in Rakhine State were reportedly among the worst, with reports of hundreds of Rohingya arbitrarily detained in prison and nonprison facilities, denied due process, and subjected to torture and abuse by Rakhine State prison and security officials.

Administration: Some prisons prevented full adherence to religious codes for prisoners, ostensibly due to space restrictions and security concerns. For example, imprisoned monks reported that authorities denied them permission to observe the Buddhist holy day, wear robes, shave their heads, or eat on a schedule compatible with the monastic code. Citing security considerations, authorities denied permission for Muslim prisoners to pray together as a group, as is the practice for Friday prayers and Ramadan. Prisoners and detainees could sometimes submit complaints to judicial authorities without censorship or negative repercussions. The International Committee of the Red Cross (ICRC) followed up with the relevant authorities on allegations of inappropriate conditions.

Independent Monitoring: The government restored the ICRC's unfettered access to prisons, prisoners, and labor camps in 2013, yet the ICRC did not have access to military or nonprison detention sites. The ICRC continued to expand its assistance to prison facilities in ethnic-minority areas, including in Shan, Kachin, and Rakhine States. Following the resumption of access, the ICRC and the government upgraded water and sanitary facilities, medical infrastructure, and waste management systems in prisons and assisted detainees in restoring or maintaining contact with family members. The ICRC reported its findings through a strictly confidential bilateral dialogue with prison authorities. These reports were neither public nor shared with any other party.

Improvements: The government continued to make systematic improvements to the country's prison system. With continued ICRC access to civilian prisons and labor camps, reports of torture have decreased while progress in overcrowding and vocational training opportunities have contributed to improvements in detention conditions and basic services.

d. Arbitrary Arrest or Detention

The law does not specifically prohibit arbitrary arrest but requires permission of a court for detention of more than 24 hours. On October 4, the government repealed the 1950 Emergency Provisions Act, used by the former regime to arrest and detain activists arbitrarily.

The law allows authorities to extend sentences after prisoners complete their original sentence, and the government used this provision. The law allows authorities to order detention without charge or trial of anyone they believe is performing or might perform any act that endangers the sovereignty and security of the state or public peace and tranquility. Authorities continued to interpret these laws broadly but used them less frequently than in past years to detain activists, student leaders, farmers, journalists, or human rights defenders.

Role of the Police and Security Apparatus

The Ministry of Home Affairs, led by a uniformed military general in accordance with the constitution, oversees the police force, which is largely responsible for law enforcement and maintenance of order in urban areas and nonconflict areas. The Defense Services oversees the Office of the Chief of Military Security Affairs (OCMSA) and plays a significant role in the maintenance of law and order, particularly in conflict areas. The Border Guard Police, under the Ministry of Home Affairs, shares responsibility for policing in northern Rakhine State with the police force.

Outside of conflict areas, security forces generally operated with respect for the rule of law, and various organizations noted the significant decrease under the new government of the pervasive and threatening influence security forces previously exerted on the lives of inhabitants. In conflict areas security forces continued to exert fear on civilians through physical abuse and threats to individual livelihoods. Public information was unavailable as to the results of any military investigations into such abuses, and generally security forces appeared to act with impunity. Legal mechanisms exist to investigate abuses by security forces but were seldom used and generally perceived to be ineffective. In one high-profile Shan State case, seven soldiers, including four officers, received five-year prison sentences with hard labor in September for the death of five civilians in June (see section 1.g.).

In Rakhine State police failed to investigate crimes motivated by intercommunal tension and in some instances discouraged family of the victims from pursuing legal action. On August 18, soldiers in Sittwe, Rakhine State, found an unconscious Rohingya woman named Raysuana outside their compound. They called village leaders to take the woman to a clinic, where she died. Clinic attendants reportedly noted injuries suggesting rape, but police refused to investigate and instead ordered villagers to bury Raysuana without a post mortem examination.

The government continued to train police on international policing standards. Foreign governments and the international community provided training on conflict-sensitive policing, community policing, crowd management, victim-centered approaches to law enforcement, and other relevant topics.

Arrest Procedures and Treatment of Detainees

While the law generally requires warrants for searches and arrests, the OCMSA and police reportedly conducted searches and made arrests at will. Special Branch police responsible for state security matters reportedly held persons during what they termed an "interrogation phase," a period not defined in law, before pretrial detention. With court permission police may detain individuals without charge for up to two weeks, with the possibility of a two-week extension.

Except in capital cases, the law does not grant detainees the right to consult an attorney or, if indigent, to have one provided by the state. In January the government passed the country's first legal aid law. The law stipulates that the Office of the Supreme Court of the Union is to manage the national legal aid scheme, with implementation overseen by a Union Legal Aid Board.

There is a functioning bail system, but bribery was a common substitute for bail. Bail is commonly offered in criminal cases. In some cases the government refused detainees the right to consult a lawyer promptly.

Arbitrary Arrest: There were reports of arbitrary arrests. In April the Arakan Liberation Party (ALP), the political wing of a cease-fire signatory ethnic armed group, published a statement accusing the military in Rakhine State of forcing civilians to act as porters and human shields. On May 5, the military filed charges of sedition and incitement under the penal code against U Khaing Myo Htun, a deputy information officer for the ALP and human rights activist. U Khaing Myo Htun reportedly gathered video documentation of the military's actions to support the public statement. He was arrested on July 25. Hundreds of supporters protested his arrest outside the courthouse at his first hearing in August. U Khaing Myo Htun remained in detention after courts denied his appeal for bail pending trial at multiple hearings, with his last hearing taking place December 2.

The government released and pardoned student leaders Zeyar Lwin and Paing Phyoe Min in April following their July 2015 arrest. The government also released the 60 persons in detention related to the 2015 Letpadan education reform protests, with all charges dropped early in the year.

<u>Pretrial Detention</u>: There were reports that authorities frequently and arbitrarily extended pretrial detentions. By law suspects may be held in pretrial detention for two weeks (with a possible two-week extension) without bringing them before a judge or informing them of the charges against them. Lawyers noted that police regularly detained suspects for the legally mandated period, failed to lodge a charge, then detained them for a series of two-week periods with trips to the judge in between. Judges and police sometimes colluded to extend detentions. According to lawyers arbitrary and lengthy pretrial detentions resulted from lengthy legal procedures, large numbers of detainees, judicial inefficiency, widespread corruption, and staff shortages.

<u>Detainee's Ability to Challenge Lawfulness of Detention before a Court</u>: The government generally did not allow detainees to challenge the legal basis of their detention in court prior to the two-week pretrial detention period.

<u>Amnesty</u>: On April 8, the president released more than 100 political detainees and on April 11, pardoned 83 political prisoners. Over the course of the year, according to human rights organizations, the government released more than 235 political prisoners through either pardon or serving their sentences and dropped charges against hundreds more.

e. Denial of Fair Public Trial

The law calls for an independent judiciary, although institutional corruption sometimes characterized the judicial system and appeared at times under the de facto control of the military and government. According to studies by civil society organizations, all level of officials received payments at all stages in the legal process for purposes ranging from routine matters, such as access to a detainee in police custody to fixing the outcome of a case. As in the previous year, the government did not take legal action against judges for corruption.

The government repealed or amended many of the laws used historically to deny individuals a fair public trial. The government repealed the Emergency Provisions Act in October. Also in October the government amended the Peaceful Assembly and Processions Act. Other laws remained on the books, including the Habitual Offenders Act, the Electronic Transactions Law, the Television and Video Act, the Law on Safeguarding the State from the Danger of Subversive Elements, and section 505(b) of the penal code, used to censor or prosecute public dissent. Provisions in the laws that allow the government to manipulate the courts for political ends remained in place, but the government used them less frequently than in previous years. It continued occasionally to use some of these laws to criminalize peaceful dissent and deprive citizens of due process and the right to a fair trial.

On January 22, the government sentenced Kachin activist Patrick Kum Jaa Lee to six months in prison for sharing a photograph on Facebook that the military deemed was defamatory. Authorities arrested Patrick in October 2015 and charged him under the 2013 Telecommunications Law. The government released him on April 1 after he finished serving his sentence in Insein Prison.

The government released Naw Ohn Hla and five other activists in April after they finished serving their sentence for protesting a land dispute in front of the Chinese embassy in Rangoon.

Trial Procedures

The law provides for the right to a fair public trial, but it also grants broad exceptions, in effect allowing the government to violate these rights at will. In ordinary criminal cases, the court generally respected some basic due process rights such as the right to an independent judiciary, public access to the courts, and the right to a defense and an appeal. Defendants do not enjoy the rights to presumption of innocence; to be informed promptly and in detail of the charges against them; to be present at their trial; to free interpretation; or, except in capital cases, to consult an attorney of their choice or have one provided at government expense. There is no right to adequate time and facilities to prepare a defense, but defense attorneys in criminal cases generally had 15 days to prepare for trial. Defendants have the right to appeal judgments, but in most appellate hearings, the original verdicts were upheld. No legal provision allows for the compelled testimony or confessions of guilt by defendants to be used in court; nonetheless, authorities reportedly engaged in both. According to local human rights lawyers, judicial violations of many of these rights and standard trial procedures declined under the new government.

Ordinary criminal cases were open to the public. While there is no right to confront witnesses and present evidence, defense attorneys could sometimes call witnesses, conduct cross-examination, and examine evidence. Defendants did not have the right to access government-held evidence, but sometimes they received access. Prodemocracy activists generally appeared able to retain counsel, but defendants' access to counsel was often inadequate. There were reports of the authorities not informing family members of the arrests of persons in a timely manner, not telling them of their whereabouts, and often denying them the right to see prisoners in a timely manner.

Concerns regarding judicial impartiality remained, and under the new government, NGOs and lawyers reported that interference in criminal trials to dictate verdicts became less common.

The government retained the ability to extend prison sentences under the law. The minister of home affairs has the authority to extend a prison sentence unilaterally by two months on six separate occasions, for a total extension of up to one year.

Political Prisoners and Detainees

The government released hundreds of political prisoners during the year. As of October only a small number of political prisoners remained in prison throughout the country, none convicted since the new government came to power. Two separate protests related to labor and land disputes in May led to more than 150 of the arrested political detainees during the year (see section 7). The government released most after a few days without conviction, while 15 individuals remained in detention awaiting trial as of December. As of December, 66 political detainees were facing trial on various charges. This number did not include detainees in Rakhine State, estimated to be in the hundreds.

Many released political prisoners experienced significant restrictions following their release, including an inability to resume studies undertaken prior to incarceration, secure travel documents, or obtain other documents related to identity or ownership of land. Under the code of criminal procedure, released political prisoners faced the prospect of serving the remainder of their sentences if rearrested for any reason.

Civil Judicial Procedures and Remedies

No specific mechanisms or laws provide for civil remedies for human rights violations; however, complainants may use provisions of the penal code and laws of civil procedure to seek civil remedies. Individuals and organizations may not appeal an adverse decision to regional human rights bodies.

Property Restitution

Under the constitution the state is the owner of all land; however, the 2012
Farmland Law allows for registration and sales of private ownership rights in land.

In January the new government formally endorsed a new land use policy following
public consultations dating to 2014. The new policy emphasizes the recognition,
protection, and registration of legitimate land tenure rights of smallholders,
communities, ethnic nationalities, women, and other vulnerable groups. It also
includes the recognition, protection, and ultimate registration of customary tenure
rights, which were not formerly legally recognized. The law allows the
government to declare land unused and assign it to foreign investors or designate it
for other uses. There is no provision for judicial review of land ownership or
confiscation decisions under either law; administrative bodies subject to political
control by the national government make final decisions on land use and
registration. Civil society groups raised concerns that the laws do not recognize
rights in traditional collective land ownership and shifting cultivation regimes,
which are particularly prevalent in upland areas inhabited by ethnic minority
groups. Acquisition of privately owned land by the government remained
governed by the 1894 Land Acquisition Act, which provides for compensation
when the government acquires land for a public purpose. Civil society groups
criticized the lack of safeguards in the law to provide payment of fair market
compensation.

Researchers had concerns that land laws, including the Farmland Law and the
Vacant, Fallow, and Virgin Land Law, facilitate land confiscation without
providing adequate procedural protections. Parallel legal frameworks and
traditional forms of land tenure in areas controlled by ethnic groups in Kachin,
Mon, Karen, and Shan States may not have formal legal recognition under the land
laws.

Parliament's Land Acquisition Investigation Commission did not have legal
authority to implement and enforce its 2013 report recommendations to return
thousands of acres of confiscated but unused land or provide compensation to
farmers from whom the government took the land, and media sources reported
little progress in returning the confiscated lands. The Vacant, Fallow, and Virgin
Land Law requires that land be returned if not used productively within four years,
but civil society groups reported that land taken by the military was left unused for
long periods.

Early in the year, the government disbanded the Land Use Management Central
Committee created in 2014 by then president Thein Sein and replaced it with the

Land Acquisition Reinspection Central Committee, with subcommittees at the state and regional, district, township, and village tract levels to continue addressing land grabbing.

There were no specific reports of returns of confiscated land throughout the year.

Under the former military regime, various government agencies--including the Myanmar Oil and Gas Enterprise, the Myanmar Ports Authority, and the army--frequently confiscated land from farmers and rural communities, generally without due process or adequate compensation. Following the attacks in October in northern Rakhine State, hundreds of homes were burned, with some reports alleging the government was the perpetrator and others alleging local Rohingya groups were to blame. The government established an investigation commission in November to acquire facts about such claims. The government did not announce plans for assistance to affected communities.

On December 22, the government sentenced 72 Shan State farmers to one month in prison for "trespassing" on land that traditionally, under customary law, belonged to those farmers. The Tatmadaw Eastern Command, which also claimed the land, pressed charges against the farmers after they rejected a compromise by which the military would formally own the land but the farmers could use it with their permission.

f. Arbitrary or Unlawful Interference with Privacy, Family, Home, or Correspondence

The law protects the privacy and security of the home and property, yet human rights organizations reported that government agents entered homes without judicial or other appropriate authorization. In September the government amended the 2012 Ward or Village Tract Administration Law, abolishing the requirement for overnight guests to register with local authorities. The new law requires registration for stays longer than one month.

The law does not protect the privacy of correspondence or other communications of citizens, and it was widely believed authorities regularly screened private correspondence, telephone calls, and e-mail. The government reportedly continued to control and monitor the licensing and procurement of all two-way electronic communication devices. The government required businesses and organizations that wished to use these devices to apply for licenses.

Activists reported that the government systematically monitored the travel of citizens and closely monitored the activities of those known to be politically active. The government did so by using the Police Special Branch, official intelligence networks, and other administrative procedures (see section 2.d.).

The law does not restrict the right of adult women and men to marry, but a 1998 Supreme Court directive prohibits legal officials from accepting petitions for marriages and from officiating over marriages between Burmese women and foreign men. The directive was sporadically enforced.

In May 2015 the government enacted the Population Control and Health Care Law, which contains provisions that could undermine protections for reproductive rights and women's rights (see section 6, Women). In August 2015 the government enacted the Buddhist Women Special Marriage law. The law stipulates notification and registration requirements for marriages between non-Buddhist men and Buddhist women. The law also introduces new obligations for non-Buddhist husbands and includes penalties for noncompliance. The Monogamy Bill, also passed in 2015, criminalizes polygamy and adultery.

In northern Rakhine State, local authorities required members of the Rohingya minority to obtain a permit to marry officially, a step not required of other ethnicities. Waiting times for the permit could exceed one year, and bribes usually were required. According to human rights organizations, on April 28, Border Guard Police in Buthidaung Township issued new instructions to village administrators outlining additional requirements for members of the Muslim community to obtain a permit to marry. The government referred to the revised procedures as "matters related to marriage of Bengali race." The new required documents included: a letter from the district immigration authorities that the couple were of legal age to marry; a letter from a station commander showing the couple was free of criminal offenses; a letter from a health assistant assuring the couple was free of communicable diseases; and a letter from village administrators confirming that the individuals were single, unmarried, and that any previous marriage was dissolved at least three years prior. Unauthorized marriages could result in prosecution of Rohingya men under the penal code, which prohibits a man from "deceitfully" marrying a woman, and could result in a prison sentence or fine. The law prohibits the adoption of children by non-Buddhist families.

g. Abuses in Internal Conflict

Incidents involving use of excessive force and other abuses in conjunction with internal conflicts occurred across the country but varied widely. In Chin State and most of the southeast, widespread and systematic violent abuses of civilian populations in ethnic minority areas continued to decline, largely due to a number of bilateral cease-fire agreements reached with ethnic armed groups. These areas also broadly fall under the Nationwide Ceasefire Agreement (NCA) signed by eight ethnic armed groups. In Kachin and Rakhine States and parts of Shan State, clashes between NCA nonsignatory groups and the government continued, with credible allegations of abuse of civilian populations by both the military and ethnic armed groups. The majority of clashes took place in northern Shan and Kachin States; however, fighting between the Arakan Army and the military in Rakhine State early in the year, as well as Rakhine violence from October through December, caused significant displacement and allegations of abuse. Conflict between ethnic armed groups themselves increased significantly, most notably in northern Shan State where the Restoration Council of Shan State fought with the Ta'ang National Liberation Army (TNLA) for much of the year. Both of these groups, and the military, were alleged to have abducted, tortured, and killed suspected combatants, burned villages, and forced civilians to porter or act as human shields.

The International Labor Organization (ILO) reported that it continued to receive reports indicating that the actual use of forced labor was decreasing overall (see section 7.b.).

In Kachin and Shan States, continuing armed clashes between the government army and ethnic armed groups displaced thousands of persons, compounding long-term displacement of conflict-affected communities in these areas.

The army continued to station forces in most ethnic armed groups' areas of influence and controlled most cities, towns, and highways. There were continued reports of widespread abuses by government soldiers and some ethnic armed groups, including killings, beatings, torture, forced labor, forced relocations, and rapes of members of ethnic groups in Shan, Kachin, and Rakhine States. Impunity for these abuses and crimes continued.

Killings: Military officials reportedly killed, tortured, and otherwise seriously abused civilians in conflict areas without public inquiry or accountability. Use of indiscriminate force also resulted in civilian deaths. Some ethnic armed groups, most notably the Restoration Council of Shan State and the TNLA, allegedly killed civilians suspected of being members of rival armed groups. Clashes between government forces and ethnic armed groups broke out periodically in northern and southern Shan State during the year, as well as in northern Rakhine State at the end of the year.

From October through December, there were numerous unconfirmed reports of unlawful killings by government security forces and by local Rohingya against civilians. On October 9, three large groups of militants (identified by the government as a group called Aqa Mul Mujahidin) attacked three Border Guard Police posts in northern Rakhine State. The attacks resulted in nine police officers dead and five wounded. The government began a security operation to search for the perpetrators, dozens of stolen arms, and more than 10,000 rounds of ammunition. In the process of these clearance operations, there were unconfirmed reports of, according to the government, approximately 100 civilian deaths, as well as 900 homes burned and approximately 30,000 displaced civilians. The tensions escalated on November 12, when clashes in northern Rakhine State resumed during a search for assailants and weapons, resulting in additional violence. On November 15, the government reported that between November 9 and November 14, the violence resulted in 69 locals and 17 security personnel killed and 234 locals arrested. There were again unconfirmed reports of abuses by security forces against Rohingya civilians, including rape, deaths, and burning of homes, as well as reports of abuses by local Rohingya against civilians. Gaining reliable information continued to be difficult as the government restricted media and humanitarian access during the continuing security situation. On November 28, the government announced the formation of a commission headed by Vice President Myint Swe to investigate reports of human rights abuses in northern Rakhine State. On December 19, the government also organized a three-day trip for 13 journalists to Maungdaw with the support of government security forces.

On June 25, soldiers in Light Battalion 362 located in Mong Yaw in northern Shan State killed five men after arresting and interrogating dozens for possible association with ethnic armed groups. Villagers discovered the bodies in shallow graves a few days later. In July the chief of military security affairs, Lieutenant General Mya Tun Oo, held a press conference admitting the army's culpability for the murders and stating the government would prosecute the perpetrators. Following an investigation, on September 13, the military held a court-martial, allowing 15 residents of the village to attend to witness the proceedings. Seven soldiers, of whom four were officers, confessed to the killings, and the military court sentenced them to five years of hard labor. During the same incident in June, soldiers reportedly killed two other men, whose bodies villagers found next to the other five. The military did not accept responsibility for those two deaths, and an investigation was pending at year's end.

Abductions: There were multiple reports of government soldiers abducting villagers in conflict areas. During a military offensive against the Shan State Army on May 18, military personnel allegedly killed two civilians and arbitrarily arrested and detained 13 civilians. One of those detained, the village chief of Wan Long, Loong Aw Aung, disappeared following his arrest. He remained missing at the end of the year.

Physical Abuse, Punishment, and Torture: NGO reports documented the military's torture and beating of civilians alleged to be working with or perceived to be sympathetic to ethnic armed groups in Kachin and Shan States. There were also continued reports of forced labor and forced recruitment by the Kachin Independence Army.

Between May 11 and May 20, the military reportedly led attacks in Kyaukme Township in Shan State. Soldiers abused, beat, and killed individuals not involved in the conflict. The Shan Human Rights Foundation reported that the military forced 48 civilians in three separate occasions to march in front of soldiers as protection for nearly 24 hours, each time without food or water. On May 14, following a battle, the military allegedly arrested, beat, and tortured five villagers using wires attached to a car battery during two nights, later forcing them to porter for the soldiers. Villagers reportedly discovered and identified the bodies of three civilians not engaged in the conflict. The government had not investigated these events by year's end.

A prominent civil society group reported that army soldiers committed numerous crimes of sexual violence against ethnic women and girls in ethnic states.

The military continued to take steps to cease forcing civilians to serve as military porters, yet unconfirmed reports continued that the military forced civilians to carry supplies or serve in other support roles in areas with outbreaks of conflict, such as northern Shan, Rakhine, and Kachin States.

Armed actors, NGOs, and civilians inside the country and operating along the border reported continued landmine use by the military and armed groups. While the government and ethnic armed groups continued to discuss joint landmine action, the discussions did not result in any joint landmine removals. The military unilaterally undertook limited landmine clearance operations in the southeast and cleared small numbers of improvised explosive devices and unexploded ordinances when identified.

The state-level Mine Risk Working Groups (MRWG) continued the process of formation, with two new groups established in June in Kayin and northern Shan States. Composed of state government representatives from various ministries, international NGOs, and local NGOs, at year's end these groups operated in Kachin, Shan, Kayah, and Kayin. In April and July, the Ministry of Social Welfare, Relief, and Resettlement's Department of Social Welfare held national-level MRWG meetings. The department also organized two union-level MRWG meetings in April and June. The department endorsed a mine risk standardized training tool, developed by MRWG members, that was available for all MRWG members to use. The department and the UN Children's Fund (UNICEF) conducted a series of training sessions throughout the year, including the first training of trainers using the new standardized tools in September.

Child Soldiers: As in previous years, there continued to be progress in implementing the 2012 joint plan of action between the government and the United Nations to cease the recruitment of child soldiers and to demobilize and rehabilitate those serving in the armed forces. As of October the UN Country Task Force on Monitoring and Reporting (CTFMR)--the official mechanism for monitoring and reporting grave violations against children--had verified only one case of child soldier recruitment. This was a significant decrease compared with the six verified cases in 2015 and 29 for 2014. The government released 101 child soldiers identified within the military's ranks, bringing the total to more than 800 child soldiers released since 2012. The military continued identifying suspected minor cases in addition to those reported by the CTFMR to the military. The CTFMR received these reports through the hotline, the forced-labor complaint mechanism, and the community-based networks. Children who fled military service or received demobilization from civil society organizations rather than through the official CTFMR process continued to face arrest and imprisonment on charges of desertion while the military investigated their cases.

The military continued enforcing its ban of all recruitment at the battalion level and continued to sanction military officers and noncommissioned personnel for complicity in child soldier recruitment and use. The military also provided information to the CTFMR that linked specific accountability measures to the respective case(s) of child recruitment or use, allowing for verification of the military's accountability measures. The military did not make these reports available to the public.

The United Nations reported that the government improved upholding its commitment under the action plan to allow UN monitors to inspect for compliance with agreed-upon procedures, to cease recruitment of children, and to implement processes for identification and demobilization of those serving in armed conflict. UN monitors were able to access all requested military installations, in both conflict- and nonconflict-affected areas, including recruitment centers, training centers, military bases, detention facilities, and border guard forces. Access to certain locations within facilities remained a periodic challenge.

The Ministry of Social Welfare, UNICEF, and other partners provided social assistance and reintegration support to discharged children.

Military officials, in cooperation with the CTFMR, continued training military officers, including recruitment officers and officers up to the rank of captain, on international humanitarian law. UNICEF trained personnel assigned to the country's four recruitment hubs and reported increased numbers of prospective child soldiers rejected at this stage. The military enhanced its recruitment procedures beginning in 2015 and continuing throughout the year, including the addition of age assessment training integrated into monthly training for recruitment personnel, as recommended by the CTFMR.

Ethnic armed groups reportedly continued to use forced recruitment and child soldiers and sometimes asked for ransom. There were multiple reports of the Kachin Independence Army forcibly recruiting members of the Taileng (also known as the Red Shan) ethnic group residing in Kachin State. Other ethnic armed groups known to recruit and use child soldiers included the Democratic Karen Benevolent Army, Karen National Liberation Army, Karen National Liberation Army Peace Council, Karenni Army, Shan State Army South, and the United Wa State Army.

Also see the Department of State's *Trafficking in Persons Report* at www.state.gov/j/tip/rls/tiprpt/.

Other Conflict-related Abuses: The government restricted the passage of relief supplies and access by international humanitarian organizations to conflict-affected areas of Rakhine, Kachin, and Shan States immediately following renewed clashes. The government regularly denied access to the United Nations and international NGOs, arguing the military could not assure the NGO workers' security or that humanitarian assistance would benefit ethnic armed group forces. In some cases the military allowed gradual access only as government forces regained control over contested areas. While locally based organizations generally had unhindered access to the 46,000 internally displaced persons (IDPs) in areas outside government control, international organizations and UN agencies could enter these areas on official missions only by following a government approval process. As of September the government had not granted humanitarian access to nongovernment controlled areas in Kachin State and only granted limited, sporadic humanitarian access in Rakhine. More than 98,000 persons remained displaced by conflict in Shan and Kachin States, and more than 120,000 in Rakhine. In some cases villagers driven from their homes fled into the forest, frequently in heavily mined areas, without adequate food, security, or basic medical care (see section 2.d.).

Following the attacks in northern Rakhine State in October, the government launched a clearance operation, including restricting all humanitarian access to Maungdaw Township. The government restored access to some parts of Maungdaw in December, but humanitarian access remained limited at the end of the year.

There were some reports of the use of civilians to shield combatants (see Physical Abuse, Punishment, and Torture).

Section 2. Respect for Civil Liberties, Including:

a. Freedom of Speech and Press

The constitution provides that "every citizen shall be at liberty in the exercise of expressing and publishing freely their convictions and opinions," but it contains the broad and ambiguous caveat that exercise of these rights must "not be contrary to the laws enacted for national security, prevalence of law and order, community peace and tranquility, or public order and morality." Threats against and arrests of journalists decreased.

Freedom of Speech and Expression: Authorities arrested, detained, convicted, and imprisoned citizens for defaming religion and expressing political opinions critical of the government, generally under the charges of protesting without a permit or violating national security laws. Prior to the government amending the law in October, some charged for demonstrating without a permit faced hundreds of court hearings and significant delays in reaching a verdict. Many individuals in urban areas, however, reported far greater freedom of speech and expression than in previous years.

On November 3, the government arrested NLD official U Myo Yan Naung Thein and charged him with defamation under the Telecommunications Law for posting comments critical of the military's response in northern Rakhine State on Facebook in October. They denied his bail in multiple hearings as he spoke out against the arbitrary nature of the Telecommunications Law. His trial was pending at the end of the year, and he remained in detention.

In April the government pardoned hundreds of political prisoners, including Htin Lin Oo, an NLD official sentenced in June 2015 to two years in prison for religious defamation. Also released were Htin Kyaw, a well-known democratic activist who spent more than a decade in prison, and five journalists from *Unity Journal*, each sentenced to 10 years in prison in 2014.

Although freedom of speech generally expanded, some persons remained wary of speaking openly about politically sensitive topics due to monitoring and harassment by security services. Police continued to monitor politicians, journalists, writers, and diplomats. Journalists complained of the widespread practice of government informants attending press conferences and other events, which they said intimidated reporters and the events' hosts. Informants demanded lists of hosts and attendees.

In October and November, instances of media self-censorship and suppression rose in connection with violence in northern Rakhine State. Media access was restricted due to the continuing security operation. Reporters and media executives were reportedly fired for printing stories critical of the military's actions in Rakhine.

<u>Press and Media Freedoms</u>: Independent media were active and increasingly able to operate with fewer restrictions. The government permitted the publication of privately owned daily newspapers. As of September authorities approved 27 dailies, seven of which were available for purchase.

Local media could cover information about human rights and political issues, including the peace process and democratic reform. The government generally permitted the media to cover protests and civil conflict, topics not reported widely in state-run media. Self-censorship continued, however, particularly on issues related to Buddhist extremism, the military, and the situation in Rakhine State. The government continued to use visas to control foreign journalists, who reported visa validities ranged from 28 days to six months. The exception to this procedure was in northern Rakhine from October through December, where the military prevented media access under the auspice of security concerns.

The military continued to practice zero-tolerance regarding perceived misreporting by the media. Authorities charged Wai Phyo, chief editor of *Daily Eleven* newspaper for defamation in a Sagaing Region court in June. A soldier sued the newspaper because of an April 2015 article that included a photograph of the soldier while noting an excursion beyond enemy lines by the military. The newspaper issued a clarification on May 4, after the army filed a complaint through the Myanmar Press Council (MPC), and sent copies of the letter to the commander in chief and to the chairperson of the army's information division. *Daily Eleven* said the army and the MPC did not respond, and the military subsequently sued the journalist a year later.

On October 31, the *Myanmar Times* newspaper fired journalist Fiona Macgregor allegedly for her reporting on allegations of human rights abuses in northern Rakhine State. Her dismissal followed criticism from President Office Spokesperson Zaw Htay on his Facebook page on October 28, following articles written by Macgregor and published in the *Myanmar Times* on October 27 and 28. Zaw Htay asserted MacGregor cited faulty sources and did not contact government officials to give them a chance to deny the allegations. In her reporting, however, MacGregor cited other outlets that quoted Zaw Htay denying the charges that abuse and rape had taken place in northern Rakhine State. Leadership at the *Myanmar Times* cited a rule in the employee handbook that staff could be fired for "denigrating the reputation of the paper" as reason for the dismissal but did not speak publicly about the firing.

Radio and television were the primary media of mass communication. Compared with previous years, circulation of independent news periodicals expanded outside of urban areas. Several print publications maintained online news websites that were popular among persons with access to the internet. The government and government-linked businesspersons controlled the content of the eight privately or quasi-governmentally owned FM radio stations.

The government continued to monopolize and control all domestic television broadcasting. It offered six public channels--five controlled by the Ministry of Information and one controlled by the armed forces. The government allowed the general population to register satellite television receivers for a fee, but the cost was prohibitive for most persons outside of urban areas. In August the ministry announced it would allow five media outlets to apply for television channel licenses as private broadcasters. Many media outlets, however, reported the costs of applying and maintaining a television channel were prohibitive.

<u>Violence and Harassment</u>: Violence and harassment of journalists dropped precipitously following the March transition to the new government. Nationalist groups, however, continued to target journalists who spoke out regarding intercommunal and Rakhine State issues. Officials continued to monitor journalists in various parts of the country.

<u>Censorship or Content Restrictions</u>: Although generally not enforced, laws prohibit citizens from electronically passing information about the country to media located outside the country, exposing journalists who reported for or cooperated with international media to potential harassment, intimidation, and arrest. There were no reports of overt prepublication censorship of press publications, and the government allowed open discussion of sensitive political and economic topics, but incidents of legal action against publications continued to raise concern among local journalists and led to some self-censorship.

On June 14, the Pazundaung Township Court in Yangon Region sentenced four individuals to one year in prison for publishing information that could cause public fear or alarm after they printed a calendar that stated "Rohingya" are an ethnic minority in the country. A fifth man charged in the case remained in hiding. Police arrested the five individuals in November 2015 after fining them approximately 1.1 million kyats ($830) each for breaking the 2014 Printing and Publication Law, which bars individuals from publishing materials that could damage national security and law and order. The court dropped the charges against the owner of the printing house.

In May 2015 the Ministry of Information filed a lawsuit against five editorial staff members of the *Daily Eleven* newspaper for allegedly defaming the ministry in a 2014 story that criticized the ministry for paying a suspiciously high price for a printing press. Editors of the *Daily Eleven* disputed the allegation and suggested that the government took legal action to stifle criticism. In June the ministry filed a contempt of court complaint against the publisher and 16 editorial employees, claiming bias in the newspaper's coverage of a court testimony given by a ministry official in the defamation case. The cases were underway as of December, and the government continued to litigate them through the end of the year.

On April 17, the government released and granted a presidential pardon to the five journalists of the *Unity Journal* newspaper whom the government had convicted in 2014 for breaching the 1923 State Secret Act.

Libel/Slander Laws: Elements of the military sued journalists on multiple occasions for what they perceived as defamation or inaccurate reporting. The government normally dropped the cases after a lengthy court process. For example, in June the military sued *7Day Daily* newspaper, accusing the media outlet of trying actively to undermine the authority of the military with a story that quoted former parliamentary speaker and retired general Thura Shwe Mann urging his colleagues from the military to work with the new government. Only after mediation by the MPC and *7Day Daily*'s published apology did the military drop the suit.

Individuals also used the Telecommunications Law to sue reporters for perceived defamation. For example, the chief minister of Rangoon, Phyo Min Thein, sued Eleven Media Group chief executive U Than Htut Aung and the editor in chief, U Wai Phyo, for defamation in November. The chief minister argued that an article insinuating he was corrupt due to an expensive wristwatch amounted to defamation.

Internet Freedom

The government did not restrict or disrupt access to the internet or censor online content. The government reportedly monitored internet communications under questionable legal authority, however, and used defamation charges to intimidate and detain some individuals using social media to criticize the military. There were also some instances of authorities intimidating online media outlets and internet users. Social media continued to be a popular forum to exchange ideas and opinions without direct government censorship. Independent research estimated internet penetration at 22 percent by fixed or mobile connection, with the number of active internet users growing by more than 350 percent between March 2015 and August. The current *Freedom on the Net* report issued by international NGO Freedom House rated internet freedom in Burma not free, but the rating increased slightly from previous years.

On February 10, the government charged Hla Hpone (accused of running the "Kyat Pha Kyi" Facebook page), under the Telecommunications Law for allegedly doctoring images of President Thein Sein and Commander in Chief Min Aung Hlaing.

Chaw Sandi Tun and Patrick Kum Ja Lee were both released after serving their six-month sentences for posting photographs on their personal Facebook accounts that authorities deemed as defaming the military.

Academic Freedom and Cultural Events

There were fewer government restrictions on academic freedom and cultural events. In its first month in office, the new government released more than 80 education activists who had been in custody for more than a year, following protests over limitations on academic freedom and association in the 2014 National Education Law. The Ministry of Education and universities demonstrated an increased willingness to collaborate with international institutions to host educational and cultural events, as well as to expand educational opportunities for undergraduate students. For example, the Yangon University of Education collaborated with the international community to hold film screenings and discussions on educational issues, while other universities worked with international institutions to allow foreign English-language instructors to teach their students full-time.

The government restricted political activity and freedom of association on university campuses by officially banning political activity on university campuses and student unions. As in previous years, the All Burma Student's Union was unable to register but participated in some activities through informal networks.

There was one reported incident of the government restricting cultural events. In June the Motion Picture Classification Board banned the showing of a film entitled *Twilight Over Burma*, which was due to open at an international human rights festival in Rangoon. The board cited concerns that the film, which tells the story of an Austrian woman who married a Shan prince and who was later arrested during the 1962 coup d'etat, could have threatened the peace process underway with ethnic armed groups. Local and international human rights organizations criticized the censorship as a violation of freedom of speech.

b. Freedom of Peaceful Assembly and Association

Freedom of Assembly

The constitution provides the right to freedom of assembly, and the government took steps to ease restrictions on these rights. On October 4, the government passed an amendment to the Peaceful Assembly and Peaceful Processions Law. The new law requires 48-hour notice to local police for any peaceful assembly or procession, removing the requirement for permission. The law also reduces the maximum penalty for conducting a peaceful assembly or procession without notice from six months to three months in prison. For second violations of the law, the maximum penalty increases to one year. Under the previous law, six-month sentences could be, and often were, stacked consecutively for every township the procession passed through, resulting in multi-year sentences; the new law allows sentencing only for the township where the assembly begins.

Citizens and international civil society groups criticized provisions of the new peaceful assembly and processions law that make it a criminal offense to give speeches that "contain false information," say anything that can harm the state, or "do anything that causes fear, a disturbance, or blocks roads, vehicles, or the public."

As part of the April 8 amnesty, the government released all prisoners involved in the March 2015 Letbadan protests. The government also released student union leaders Kyaw Ko Ko and Lin Htet Naing, whom they had arrested in October and November 2015.

Farmers and social activists continued to hold protests over land rights and older cases of land confiscation throughout the country, and human rights groups continued to report some cases in which the government arrested groups of farmers and those supporting them for demanding the return of confiscated land. Many reported cases involved land taken by the army under the former military regime and given to private companies or individuals with ties to the military. Common charges used to convict the peaceful protesters included criminal trespass, violation of the Peaceful Assembly and Processions Act, and violation of section 505(b) of the penal code, which criminalizes actions that the government deemed likely to cause "an offence against the State or against the public tranquility." The Assistance Association for Political Prisoners (Burma) reported more than 100 arrests and indictments during the year, with approximately 116 individuals, including farmers and laborers, known to be facing trial.

Freedom of Association

While the constitution and laws allow citizens to form associations and organizations, the government sometimes restricted this right. The former government reportedly blocked efforts of ethnic language and literature associations to meet and teach, and it impeded efforts of Islamic and Christian associations and other organizations to gather and preach. The new government did not address these restrictions as of November.

In 2014 the government adopted the Law Relating to Registration of Organizations, which effectively voided State Law and Order Restoration Council Law 6/1988. The 2014 registration law stipulates voluntary registration for local NGOs and removes punishments for noncompliance for both local and international NGOs.

Activists reported that civil society groups, community-based organizations, and informal networks operated openly and continued to discuss openly human rights and other political problems.

c. Freedom of Religion

See the Department of State's *International Religious Freedom Report* at www.state.gov/religiousfreedomreport/.

d. Freedom of Movement, Internally Displaced Persons, Protection of Refugees, and Stateless Persons

The law does not explicitly and comprehensively protect freedom of internal movement, foreign travel, emigration, and repatriation. Laws provide rights for citizens to settle and reside anywhere in the country "according to law." Laws related to noncitizens empower the president to make rules for the purpose of requiring registration of foreigners' movements and authorize officials to require registration for every temporary change of address exceeding 24 hours.

In-country Movement: Regional and local orders, directives, and instructions restricted freedom of movement. In September the government amended the 2012 Ward or Village Tract Administration Law, removing the requirement that persons who intend to spend the night at a place other than their registered domicile inform local ward or village authorities in advance. The new law requires that guests inform local authorities only if their stay outside their registered domicile is longer than one month.

The government restricted the ability of IDPs and stateless persons to move. While a person's possession of identification documents primarily related to their freedom of movement, authorities also considered race, ethnicity, religion, and place of origin as factors in enforcing these regulations. Residents of ethnic-minority states reported that the government restricted the travel of, involuntarily confined, and forcibly relocated IDPs and stateless persons.

Restrictions on in-country movement of Muslims in Rakhine State were extensive. Authorities required the Rohingya, a stateless population, to carry special documents and travel permits for internal movement in five areas in Rakhine State where the Rohingya ethnic minority primarily resides: Buthidaung, Maungdaw, Rathedaung, Kyauktaw, and Sittwe (see Stateless Persons). Township officers in Buthidaung and Maungdaw townships continued to require Rohingya to submit a "form for informing absence from habitual residence" for permission to stay overnight in another village and to register on the guest list with the village administrator. Obtaining these forms and permits often involved extortion and bribes.

Restrictions governing the travel of foreigners, Rohingya, and others between townships in northern Rakhine State varied, depending on township, and usually required submission of a document known as "Form 4." A traveler could obtain this form only from the Township Immigration and National Registration Department (INRD) and only if that person provided an original copy of a family list, temporary registration card, and two guarantors. Travel authorized under Form 4 is valid for 14 days. The cost to obtain the form varied from township to township, with payments required to village administrators or to the township INRD office in amounts ranging from 50,000 to 100,000 kyats ($38 to $76). Change of residency from one village or township to another in northern Rakhine State required permission from the INRD or the township, district, and state officials. While Rohingya could change residency, the government would not register them on a new household registration list in that new location. This practice effectively prevented persons from changing residency.

On March 28, the President's Office lifted the state of emergency in Rakhine State that had been in place since 2012. This act did not improve freedom of movement for IDPs and stateless persons, since local administrative orders restricting those freedoms stem from separate legislation. Township administrators in Maungdaw and Buthidaung in northern Rakhine State reinforced this circumstance by announcing in April that the curfew order would remain in place until further notice.

Travel restrictions effectively prevented Muslims from northern Rakhine State from traveling outside of the state. There were reports of the government preventing Rohingya living outside Rakhine State from traveling into the northern part of the state.

There were reports of regular, unannounced nighttime household checks in northern Rakhine State and in other areas.

Foreign Travel: The government reduced restrictions preventing foreign travel of political activists, former political prisoners, and some local staff of foreign embassies. While some administrative restrictions remained, local organizations reported encountering far fewer delays and restrictions. Stateless persons, particularly the Rohingya, were unable to obtain documentation necessary for foreign travel.

Exile: There was a sizeable diaspora, with some citizens choosing to remain outside the country after years of self-imposed exile. During the year the government encouraged exiles to help rebuild their country, and some returned home.

Emigration and Repatriation: According to the Office of UN High Commissioner for Refugees (UNHCR), as of the end of September, the verified population of concern for UNHCR and the Thai Ministry of Interior, including those who were unregistered, was 103,366. The government allowed UNHCR and other organizations limited access to monitor potential areas of return to assess conditions for the eventual voluntary return of refugees and IDPs.

UNHCR reported nearly 33,000 registered Rohingya refugees lived in two official camps, Kutapalong and Nayapara, in Cox's Bazar district in southeastern Bangladesh, with approximately 35,000 undocumented Rohingya living adjacent to the two camps in makeshift settlements. An additional 200,000 to 500,000 undocumented Rohingya were living outside the camps among the local host population in the surrounding towns and villages. Neither Bangladesh nor Burma claimed the stateless Rohingya as citizens. In Malaysia UNHCR registered approximately 54,400 Rohingya, of whom approximately 13,300 were asylum seekers and 41,100 were refugees. NGOs believed there were many more unregistered Rohingya in Malaysia. At the end of September, the total number of registered asylum seekers and refugees from Burma in Malaysia was 150,226, including more than 41,000 Chin and 39,000 non-Rohingya Burmese Muslims and other ethnic groups from Burma.

According to the United Nations, in the first half of the year, mixed maritime movements of refugees and migrants through Southeast Asia were limited to isolated attempts by several hundred persons trying to reach Malaysia and Australia, fewer than during the first six months of any year since 2011.

Internally Displaced Persons

There were an estimated 220,000 persons displaced by violence in Rakhine and Kachin States and northern Shan State. This figure did not include the southeast, where estimates ranged from between 100,000 and 400,000 persons displaced due to prolonged armed conflict in those areas. Accurate figures were difficult to determine due to poor access to affected areas.

As of September the UN Office of Coordination for Humanitarian Affairs estimated that more than 100,000 persons remained displaced because of continued armed conflict in Kachin and Shan States. Camps housing more than half of the IDPs were located in areas beyond government control where government forces restricted humanitarian access. There were approximately 172 locations hosting IDPs. Some IDPs found refuge with hosting families, and others hid in forested areas straddling the border with China.

Fighting between government forces and ethnic armed groups continued in Kachin, Shan, Karen, and Rakhine States. Ethnic armed groups also clashed among themselves in northern Shan State. Access to displaced persons continued to be a challenge, with the government restricting access by humanitarian actors to provide aid to affected communities. In Shan State, of the 80,000 displaced by the prior conflict, local and international relief agencies reported more than 42,000 had returned. Following November attacks by ethnic armed groups on security forces in Shan State, many displaced persons crossed into China, with the UN Office for Coordination of Humanitarian Affairs estimating them at 15,000 at that time. Since mid-April circumscribed fighting between the military and the Arakan Army displaced approximately 1,500 persons in Buthidaung, Kyawktaw, Ponnagyun, and Rathedaung townships in Rakhine State. The government relocated the displaced, who initially stayed in schools, to areas where they could build makeshift shelters within their displaced communities.

Armed clashes between a faction of the Democratic Karen Buddhist Army and the Border Guard Police in September led to more than 5,600 IDPs from 22 villages taking refuge in Myaing Gyi Ngu Township (two hours north of Karen State's capital Hpa An). Additional estimates of up to 2,000 persons sought shelter in border areas and stayed with host communities. A number of local and community-based actors provided support and assistance, including youth groups, faith-based organizations, and private donors. International actors provided support, in coordination with their government counterparts.

Approximately 120,000 persons, including Rohingya and Kaman Muslims, and ethnic Rakhine remained displaced in Rakhine State following the 2012 violence, and reports estimated that security operations in northern Rakhine displaced 30,000 persons. Nearly 90,000 Rohingya IDPs lived in Sittwe's rural camps, where they relied on assistance from aid agencies. Humanitarian agencies provided access to clean water, food, shelter, and sanitation in most IDP camps. The government limited health and education services and livelihood opportunities through systematic restrictions on movement. Rakhine State authorities and security officials imposed severe and disproportionate restrictions on movements of Rohingya IDPs. Conditions in Aung Mingalar, the sole remaining Muslim quarter in Sittwe, remained poor, with Rohingya allowed to leave the fenced and guarded compound to shop for necessities at nearby markets or to visit outside health clinics if they paid a fee to security services. There were reports that some Rohingya were able to engage in limited commercial activities outside Aung Mingalar. While restrictions on movement remained in place, local residents reported some easing of restrictions on their movements.

During the year humanitarian agencies more regularly received travel authorizations to provide assistance, but humanitarian access to Rakhine State was irregular and often restricted. Humanitarian workers continued to be under pressure from local communities to reduce assistance to Muslim IDPs and villages, despite limited adequate access to meet humanitarian need.

UNHCR noted some small-scale, spontaneous IDP returns in the southeast of the country.

Protection of Refugees

Access to Asylum: The country's laws do not provide for the granting of asylum or refugee status, and the government has not established a system for providing protection to refugees.

UNHCR did not register any asylum seekers during the year.

Stateless Persons

The Myanmar Population and Housing Census reported that there were an estimated 1.09 million Muslims residing in Rakhine State who were stateless because of discriminatory provisions in the country's 1982 Citizenship Law. The census did not enumerate the Rohingya population in specific due to their statelessness, but according to UNHCR the census number was an accurate estimate of the stateless Rohingya Muslims in Rakhine State. Based on preliminary analysis, there were likely significant numbers of stateless persons and persons with undetermined nationality throughout the country, including persons of Chinese, Indian, and Nepali descent.

Provisions of the Citizenship Law relating to the acquisition of citizenship discriminate on the grounds of race or ethnicity and contributed to statelessness. Following the entry into force of the 1982 law and procedures, the government released a list of 135 recognized "national ethnic groups" whose members, according to the law, are automatically "citizens." The government list of 135 official ethnic groups excluded the Rohingya, and subsequent actions by the government rendered members of the Rohingya ethnic minority stateless. The law defines "national ethnic group" only as a racial and ethnic group that can prove origins in the country back to 1823, the year prior to British colonization. Several ethnic minority groups, including the Chin and Kachin, criticized the classification system as inaccurate. While the majority of the country's inhabitants automatically acquired citizenship under these provisions, some minority groups, including the Rohingya; persons of Indian, Chinese, and Nepali descent; and "Pashu" (Straits Chinese), some of whose members had previously enjoyed citizenship in the country, are not included on the government's list. The law does not provide protection for children born in the country who do not have a "relevant link" to another state. As a result statelessness continued to increase, since children of stateless parents could not acquire citizenship. UNHCR and a number of human rights and humanitarian organizations continued to advocate amendment of the Citizenship Law to bring it in line with the country's international human rights obligations and commitments (see section 6, Children).

The name Rohingya is used in reference to a group that self-identifies as belonging to an ethnic group defined by religious, linguistic, and other ethnic features. Rohingya do not dispute their ethnogeographic origins from present day Bangladesh, but they hold that they have resided in what is now Rakhine State for decades, if not centuries. Previously authorities usually referred to Rohingya pejoratively as "Bengali," claiming that the Muslim residents of northern Rakhine State are irregular migrants from Bangladesh or descendants of migrants transplanted by the British during colonial rule. In May the government policy began using "Muslims in Rakhine State" to refer to the population. In May the government announced a plan to continue its citizenship verification process in Rakhine State by continuing to issue Identity Cards for Nationality Verification (ICNV). As of December the government issued ICNVs to 3,162 of the 390,000 Kaman Muslims and Rohingya, who surrendered their previous national identity card--the Temporary Identity Certificate--in 2015 at the government's request. The government no longer requires all participants to identify as "Bengali" as a condition of participating in the process, nor does it require applicants to list their race or religion on forms in the earliest phases of the process. As of December an estimated 2,000 Rohingya participated in the new government's citizen verification process, applying for ICNV as a first step. As of December the government had not released results, and individuals going through the process had not enjoyed any additional benefits in recognition of their participation. The government continued to call Rohingya to participate, but many of them expressed the need for more assurances about the results of the process. Many said the government once recognized them as citizens but expressed fear the government would either not grant them citizenship or would grant them a form of lesser citizenship, curtailing their rights.

According to the Citizenship Law, two lesser forms of citizenship exist: associate and naturalized. According to other legal statutes, these citizens are unable to run for political office; serve in the military, law enforcement, or public administration; inherit land or money; or pursue certain professional degrees, such as medicine and law. According to the Citizenship Law, only the third generation of associate or naturalized citizens are able to acquire full citizenship.

Rohingya experienced severe legal, economic, and social discrimination. The government required them to receive prior approval for travel outside their village of residence; limited their access to higher education, health care, and other basic services; and prohibited them from working as civil servants, including as doctors, nurses, or teachers. Authorities singled out Rohingya in northern Rakhine State to perform forced labor and arbitrarily arrested them. Authorities required Rohingya to obtain official permission for marriages and limited the registration of children to two per family, but local enforcement of the two-child policy was inconsistent. For the most part, authorities registered additional children beyond the two-child limit for Rohingya families, yet there were cases of authorities not doing so.

Restrictions impeded the ability of Rohingya to construct houses or religious buildings.

Local security officials in Rakhine State committed violent crimes and arbitrarily arrested an unknown number of Rohingya, according to reports. Many of these reports occurred during October to December following attacks against police and border authorities by local groups and a subsequent security clearance operation. The perpetrators and the reported abuses remained unconfirmed at year's end.

The number of voluntary migrants departing Rakhine State dropped to its lowest since 2011, with only a few hundred departures reported in the first six months of the year. This significantly reduced the risk to Rohingya migrants who had been vulnerable to human trafficking, migrant smuggling, and other abuses once on boats and during transit. Following violent attacks against Border Guard Police posts on October 9, however, UN and NGO reports estimated more than 20,000 persons in northern Rakhine State began to move across the Bangladeshi border to flee security operations underway in the area.

There were reports of extrajudicial killings, rape, sexual violence, arbitrary detention, forced labor, sex trafficking, torture, mistreatment in detention, deaths in custody, and systematic denial of due process and fair trial rights in Rakhine State.

According to media reports and local NGOs, on January 11 in Shwe Zar Kat Pa Kaung Village, Maungdaw Township, villagers found the bodies of two young men, reportedly including one minor, in a boat the day after they went fishing. Villagers noted that they last saw the two near a Border Guard Police station, but no investigation took place and the perpetrators were unknown at year's end.

Local organizations reported 24 cases of arbitrary arrest and detention in Rakhine State, mostly in Buthidaung Township. Most of the individuals detained by the government secured their release by payment of up to 950,000 kyat ($715). A number of those arrested reported authorities beat them while in prison. One man arrested on April 5 in Buthidaung Township reported that officials handcuffed and tied him to the roof of the prison, where they slapped, punched, and beat him and set his chest on fire. Officials released him following payment of 10 million kyat ($7,500). Local NGOs reported widely credible incidents of forced labor, most allegedly perpetrated by the Tatmadaw and the Border Guard Police. Government officials reportedly used villagers for maintenance work and were either unpaid or received compensation that was well below market rates.

Section 3. Freedom to Participate in the Political Process

The constitution provides the ability for citizens to choose their government through elections held by secret ballot, although certain provisions prevent it from being a fully representational system and assuring the free expression of the will of the people. Constitutional provisions grant one-quarter of all national and regional parliamentary seats to active-duty military appointees and provide the military authority to appoint the ministers of defense, home affairs, and border affairs and indefinitely assume power over all branches of the government should the president declare a national state of emergency. A separate constitutional provision prohibits persons with immediate relatives with foreign citizenship from becoming president. Amending the constitution requires more than 75 percent approval by members of parliament, giving the military veto power over the constitutional amendment process.

Elections and Political Participation

Recent Elections: Final reports from international observers stated that they found no irregularities in more than 90 percent of polling stations during the November 2015 general elections. Observers considered the elections to be generally reflective of the will of the people, notwithstanding some structural shortcomings. Observers raised concerns that a large number of unelected seats in parliament were reserved for military officers, that some candidates were disqualified on a discriminatory basis, and that almost all members of the Rohingya community, many of whom voted in previous elections, were disenfranchised. The NLD, chaired by Aung San Suu Kyi, won 77.1 percent of the contested 1,150 seats at the state, regional, and union levels and officially opened parliament in January. The NLD-led parliament elected Htin Kyaw as president.

Political Parties and Political Participation: Opposition parties and civil society organizations continued to exercise and expand their rights to assemble and protest.

Participation of Women and Minorities: No laws limit the participation of women and members of minorities in the political process, and women and minorities did so. Nevertheless, women and minorities continued to be underrepresented in government. Aung San Suu Kyi was the only woman in a cabinet of 22 ministers serving at the national level. There were 43 women in the 440-seat lower house of parliament, 23 in the 224-seat upper house of parliament, and 79 among the 882 members in the seven state and seven regional parliaments. The representation of women at both the national and the state and regional levels was more than 10 percent among elected representatives. Women lead two subnational governments, including the chief ministers of Kayin State and Tanintharyi region.

As of December five ministers of the seven ethnic states belonged to the ethnic groups of their states. There were 37 representatives from ethnic parties in the lower house of parliament, 18 in the upper house, and 77 representatives from among the 882 state and region parliamentarians. The representation of ethnic minority parliamentarians from ethnic minority political parties at both the national, state, and regional level was approximately 11 percent. These figures from all levels did not account for ethnic minority members of the National League for Democracy or Union Solidarity and Development Party, the former of which included numerous ethnic members, although no clear statistics existed.

Rohingya continued to be excluded from the political process, as their political rights (whether to vote or run for office) remained severely curtailed. While Rohingya consist of approximately a third of the population in Rakhine State, there were no Rohingya representatives in the state parliament.

Section 4. Corruption and Lack of Transparency in Government

The law provides criminal penalties for corruption by officials, and the government continued efforts to curb rampant corruption. The government began its term by taking a vocal and public stand against corruption, including by instituting new restrictions on the gifts civil servants can accept. The government's anticorruption efforts, however, were limited because parts of government remained outside the government's direct control, including for General Administration Department.

Corruption: Corruption remained a problem, particularly in the judiciary. Police reportedly often required victims to pay substantial bribes for criminal investigations and routinely extorted money from the civilian population. Nevertheless, the government took some steps to investigate and address corruption of government officials.

Financial Disclosure: Public officials were not subject to public financial disclosure laws. The law requires the president and vice presidents to furnish a list of family assets to the speaker of the joint houses of parliament, and the law requires persons appointed by the president to furnish a list of personal assets to the president. The government did not make the reports available to the public.

In April the President's Office issued guidelines outlining new rules for civil servants on the types and amounts of permissible gifts. Under the new guidelines, civil servants cannot accept gifts worth more than 25,000 kyats ($18), a much lower threshold than the 300,000 kyats ($225) limit under the previous administration. The rules also require civil servants to report all offers of gifts to their supervisors, whether or not they are accepted. Separately, the government widely publicized the apparent attempt by a media company to bribe an assistant of a senior government official during a public festival in mid-April.

Public Access to Information: The law does not provide for public access to information; however, the government undertook several programs or initiatives to increase fiscal transparency. The union government's enacted budget was publicly available, but the public saw only summary information for each ministry with the broader government privy to ministry details. The government increased greatly its presence on social media, and nearly all ministries and both houses of parliament had active Facebook pages used as a primary channel of information.

Dedicated channels broadcast parliamentary activity. Unlike in previous years, the government made some voting records of parliamentarians available to the public.

Section 5. Governmental Attitude Regarding International and Nongovernmental Investigation of Alleged Violations of Human Rights

The government did not fully allow domestic human rights organizations to function independently. As of year's end, the current government had not fulfilled the previous government's 2012 pledge to open an office of the UN Office of the High Commissioner for Human Rights (OHCHR). While allowing the OHCHR to maintain a nominal presence in country, the government delayed visa issuance for some OHCHR staff members and continued to require travel authorization for travel to Rakhine State. Human rights NGOs were able to open offices and operate with less harassment and monitoring by authorities than in previous years.

Human rights activists and advocates, including representatives from international NGOs, continued to obtain short-term visas that required them to leave the country periodically for renewal. The government continued to monitor the movements of foreigners and interrogated citizens concerning contacts with foreigners, but observers reported a decrease in such activity in some areas.

The United Nations or Other International Bodies: During the year there was a significant deterioration in access for UN and international humanitarian organizations, particularly in Rakhine and nongovernment-controlled areas where there were clashes with ethnic armed groups. Beginning in April the military blocked access to areas outside government control in Kachin State and instructed IDPs in these areas to cross conflict lines and travel to designated distribution points in government areas to collect necessary relief supplies. The government did not regularly grant approval for humanitarian convoys, but smaller scale missions conducted by individual and local agencies reportedly were more successful in obtaining approvals. UN agencies, along with all other humanitarian actors, were not able to access northern Rakhine State from October to December, following the attacks and subsequent security response.

The government facilitated regular visits of the UN special rapporteur for human rights in Myanmar and the UN special adviser to the secretary-general, but it had not come to an agreement with the OHCHR on the establishment of a field office within the country.

Following a 2012 government pledge to allow the ICRC prison access, the ICRC had full access to independent civilian prisons and labor camp visits. The government also allowed the ICRC to operate in ethnic-minority states, including in Shan, Rakhine, and Kachin States.

Government Human Rights Bodies: The Myanmar National Human Rights Commission (MNHRC) investigated incidents of gross human rights abuses and in some instances called on the government to hold accountable members of the police force or military implicated in the crimes. Its ability to operate as a credible, independent mechanism remained limited. The commission supported the development of human rights education curricula, distributed human rights materials, and conducted human rights training. It engaged with the United Nations and international partners and increasingly with civil society.

Despite this progress, in June the MNHRC came under significant public scrutiny over its mediation of a human rights case in Rangoon. Reporter Ko Swe Win published a story of two teenage female housekeepers who had been tortured, abused, and isolated from any outside contact at a Rangoon tailoring shop over the course of five years. When police took no action in July, Win brought the case to the MNHRC, which proceeded to handle the case through mediation, facilitating a payment of approximately 5.45 million kyat ($4,100) to the victims from the alleged abusers--4.1 million kyat ($3,100) to one family and 1.35 million kyat ($1,000) to the other. Public outrage ensued over the lack of formal prosecution and for a perceived failure on behalf of the MNHRC to defend the rights of the victims. Led by the antihuman trafficking unit, police subsequently arrested three alleged abusers on September 20 and 21 and reportedly charged them under the Antihuman Trafficking Law. Following this incident parliament called for a review of the MNHRC, and four MNHRC commissioners voluntarily resigned. The review continued at year's end. The government awarded journalist Ko Swe Win a commendation for his work on September 23.

In August the government established the Advisory Commission on Rakhine State, headed by Kofi Annan, as a neutral and impartial body tasked with proposing concrete measures to improve the welfare of all persons in Rakhine State. The commission visited Rakhine State twice during the year, both before and after the violence in Rakhine broke out in October, and their recommendations were due to the government in early 2017.

Section 6. Discrimination, Societal Abuses, and Trafficking in Persons

Women

Rape and Domestic Violence: Rape is illegal but remained a significant problem, and the government did not enforce the law effectively. Spousal rape is not a crime unless the wife is under 14 years of age. The government did not release statistics concerning the number of rape prosecutions and convictions. Police generally investigated reported cases of rape, but there were reports that police investigations were not sensitive to victims. One prominent women's group reported that police in some cases verbally abused women who reported rape and that women could be sued for impugning the dignity of the perpetrator, especially in Karen and Mon States.

Domestic violence against women, including spousal abuse, remained a serious problem. Abuse within families was prevalent and considered socially acceptable. Spousal abuse or domestic violence was difficult to measure because the government did not maintain statistics. According to media reports, there were 700 cases of rape reported annually; however, statistics to verify this estimate were not available. There are laws that prohibit committing bodily harm against another person, but there are no laws specifically against domestic violence or spousal abuse, including spousal rape of women above 13 years of age. Punishment for violating the law includes prison terms ranging from one year to life, in addition to possible fines.

There were reports of rape by military and security officials in Kachin, Shan, and Rakhine States. The military rejected all allegations that rape was an institutionalized practice in the military but admitted in 2014 that its soldiers had committed 40 known rapes of civilian women since 2011. While there was no reliable estimate for rape cases nationwide, civil society groups observed an increase in the number of cases reported during the year.

Female Genital Mutilation/Cutting (FGM/C): There were no reports of FGM/C practiced in the country.

Sexual Harassment: The penal code prohibits sexual harassment and imposes fines or up to one year's imprisonment for verbal harassment and up to two years' imprisonment for physical contact. Civil society organizations reported that efforts to address sexual harassment revealed that most men and women were unaware of laws that prohibit sexual harassment, nor could they provide examples of enforcement. Additionally, there was no information on the prevalence of the problem because these crimes were largely unreported. Local civil society organizations reported that police investigators were not sensitive to victims and rarely followed through with investigations or prosecutions.

Reproductive Rights: Couples and individuals generally have the right to decide the number, spacing, and timing of children. In May 2015 the government enacted the Population Control and Health Care Law, which contains provisions that, if put into effect, could undermine protections for reproductive and women's rights, including imposing birth-spacing requirements. Under the law the president or the national government may designate "special regions" for health care following consideration of factors such as population, natural resources, birth rates, and food availability. Once a special region is declared, the government allows the creation of special health-care organizations to perform various tasks, including establishing regulations related to family planning methods. The government had not designated any such special regions since the law's enactment. In September a lower-house lawmaker requested that the government implement the Population Control and Health Care Law to restrict the birth rates for Muslim communities in two northern Rakhine State townships (Maungdaw and Buthidaung). The Union health minister rejected the request.

A two-child local order issued by the state government of Rakhine pertaining to the Rohingya population in two northern townships remained in effect, but the government and NGOs reported it was not enforced (see section 1.f.). The government was expanding the availability of different types of contraceptives in both government and private-sector clinics. Nonetheless, only 50 percent of women between the ages of 15 and 49 were using a modern method of contraceptives, and 16 percent of women had an unmet need for family planning, according to current UN Population Fund (UNFPA) estimates. Access to family planning was limited in rural areas, and local organizations noted that the unmet need for family planning was particularly high in Rakhine. A lack of commodities and security concerns in conflict-affected regions also affected access to family planning.

According to UN estimates, the maternal mortality ratio nationwide was 178 deaths per 100,000 live births. There were 1,700 maternal deaths in 2015, and the lifetime risk of maternal death was one in 260. According to the 2014 national census, the maternal mortality rate in Rakhine State was 314 deaths per 100,000 live births, the fifth highest among states/regions. NGOs reported that humanitarian access and movement restrictions among the Rohingya limited access to health-care services and contributed to higher maternal mortality rates in Rakhine, compared with the national average. Complications resulting from unsafe abortion were also a leading cause of maternal deaths. The law prohibits abortion except to save a woman's life. Other major factors influencing maternal mortality included poverty; limited availability of and access to comprehensive sexual and reproductive health services and information, including contraception, and maternal and newborn health services; a high number of home births; and the lack of access to services from appropriately trained and skilled birth attendants, midwives, auxiliary midwives, basic health staff, and other trained community health workers. UNFPA estimated that skilled health personnel attended only 71 percent of births.

Discrimination: By law women enjoy the same legal status and rights as men, including property and inheritance rights and religious and personal status, but it was not clear if the government enforced the law. The law requires equal pay for equal work, but it was not clear if the formal sector respected this requirement. Women remained underrepresented in most traditionally male occupations (mining, forestry, carpentry, masonry, and fishing) and remained effectively barred from certain professions. Poverty affected women disproportionately. Within the antidiscrimination provision in the constitution regarding appointing civil service personnel, the law qualifies its nondiscrimination based on sex by stating that nothing shall prevent the appointment of men to "positions that are suitable for men only," with no further definition of what "suitable for men only" constitutes. The military continued to accept women into its Defense Services Academy.

Customary law was widely used to address issues of marriage, property, and inheritance, and it differs from the provisions under statutory law.

Children

Birth Registration: The 1982 Citizenship Law automatically confers full citizenship status to 135 recognized national ethnic groups as well as to persons who met citizenship requirements under previous citizenship legislation. Moreover, the government confers full citizenship to second-generation children of both parents with any form of citizenship, as long as at least one parent has full citizenship. Third-generation children of associate or naturalized citizens can acquire full citizenship. Residents derive full citizenship through parents, both of whom must be one of the 135 officially recognized "national races" according to the Citizenship Law. Under the law the government does not officially recognize Rohingya as an ethnic group and consider them stateless. While some of the Rohingya participating in the citizenship verification process (see section 2.d.) may obtain a form of naturalized citizenship, the government did not make explicit which citizenship rights Rohingya would have through the program. It remained unclear if a member of an unrecognized ethnic group granted a form of citizenship through the program would be able to transmit a form of citizenship to their children.

A prominent international NGO noted significant rural-urban disparities in birth registration. In major cities (for example, Rangoon and Mandalay), births were registered immediately. In larger cities parents must register births to qualify for basic public services and obtain national identification cards. In smaller towns and villages, birth registration often was informal or nonexistent.

A birth certificate provided important protections for children, particularly against child labor, early marriage, and recruitment into the armed forces and armed groups. Sometimes a lack of birth registration, but more often a lack of availability, complicated access to public services in remote communities. For the Rohingya community, birth registration was a significant problem (see section 2.d.). While the practice of "blacklisting" some Rohingya children ceased following the dissolution of the NaSaKa border guard force in 2013(an inter-agency force established in 1992 and comprised of approximately 1,200 immigration, police, intelligence and customs officials that operated near the Bangladesh border), human rights organizations reported that early in the year, an additional 15 children were blacklisted in Rathedaung, meaning the children were not included in the household and family registration list (see section 2.d.).

<u>Education</u>: By law education is compulsory, free, and universal through the fourth grade (approximately age 10). The government continued to allocate minimal resources to public education, and schools charged informal fees. Many child rights activists in Rangoon noted that such fees were decreasing and were less often mandatory. There was little reported difference between girls and boys in attendance rates.

Local and international observers considered the 2015 National Education Law an improvement over past legislation, but local and international civil society continued to point out that it does not legalize student unions and lacks mandated national funding for the education sector.

Education access for internally displaced and stateless children remained limited.

<u>Child Abuse</u>: Laws prohibit child abuse, but they were neither adequate nor enforced. NGOs reported corporal punishment being widely used against children as a means of discipline. The punishment for violations is up to two years' imprisonment or a fine of up to 10,000 kyats ($7.50). There was anecdotal evidence from the field of violence against children occurring within families, schools, in situations of child labor and exploitation, and in armed conflict. The Ministry of Social Welfare, with the support of UNICEF and international NGOs, expanded its social work case management child protection pilot programs in 10 new townships, bringing the total to 27, to provide more caseworkers and support services for child victims of sexual and physical violence. Since the work started, the Department of Social Welfare received more than 1,200 cases of violence, abuse, and neglect of children and responded with social work visits and services. In Rakhine State continued violence left many families and children displaced or with restrictions on their movement, which in turn exposed them to an environment of violence and exploitation. Armed conflict in Kachin and Shan States had a similar effect on children in those areas.

<u>Early and Forced Marriage</u>: The law stipulates the minimum age requirement for marriage is 15 years old, but child marriage still occurred. According to the 2014 census, 13.2 percent of females reported to have been married between the ages of 15 and 19. There were no reliable statistics on forced marriage. A review conducted by a UN organization in February found that child marriage remained an important and underaddressed problem in rural areas. The census data showed that Shan, Kayah, and Chin States had the highest rates of child marriage in the country.

<u>Female Genital Mutilation/Cutting (FGM/C)</u>: Information is provided in the women's section above.

<u>Sexual Exploitation of Children</u>: There was no verifiable data on the commercial sexual exploitation of children, either inside or outside the country. Children were subjected to sex trafficking in the country, and a small number of foreign child sex tourists exploited children. The law does not explicitly prohibit child sex tourism, but the 1949 Suppression of Prostitution Act and the Prostitution Act prohibit pimping and prostitution, respectively, and the penal code prohibits having sex with a minor under the age of 14. The penalty for the purchase and sale of commercial sex acts from a child under age 18 is 10 years' imprisonment. The Child Law prohibits pornography, the penalty for which is two years' minimum imprisonment and a fine of 10,000 kyats ($7.50). The law prohibits statutory rape; if a victim is under 14 years of age, the law considers the sexual act rape with or without consent. The maximum sentence for statutory rape is two years' imprisonment when the victim is between ages 12 and 14, and 10 years' to life imprisonment when the victim is under 12.

<u>Displaced Children</u>: The mortality rate of internally displaced children in conflict areas was significantly higher than in the rest of the country (see section 2.d., Internally Displaced Persons).

<u>International Child Abductions</u>: The country is not a party to the 1980 Hague Convention on the Civil Aspects of International Child Abduction. See the Department of State's *Annual Report on International Parental Child Abduction* at travel.state.gov/content/childabduction/en/legal/compliance.html.

Anti-Semitism

There was one synagogue in Rangoon serving a small Jewish congregation. There were no reports of anti-Semitic acts.

Trafficking in Persons

See the Department of State's *Trafficking in Persons Report* at www.state.gov/j/tip/rls/tiprpt/.

Persons with Disabilities

The government passed a disability law in June 2015 to prohibit discrimination against persons with physical, sensory, hearing, intellectual, and mental disabilities in employment, education, access to health care, the judicial system, or in the provision of other state services. The law does not specifically prohibit discrimination against persons with disabilities in air travel and other forms of transportation, but it directs the government to assure that persons with disabilities have easy access to public transportation. The government was still in the process of drafting implementation guidelines for the disability law and did not effectively enforce these provisions.

The Ministry of Health is responsible for medical rehabilitation of persons with disabilities, and the Ministry of Social Welfare, Relief, and Resettlement is responsible for vocational training, education, and social protection strategies. During the year the government recognized the Myanmar Federation of Persons with Disabilities (formerly known as the Myanmar Council of Persons with Disabilities) to serve as an umbrella group for disabled persons organizations. The National Committee on Disability is the ministerial committee charged with promoting the rights of persons with disabilities. It did not convene during the year.

According to the Myanmar Physical Handicap Association, a significant number of military personnel, armed group members, and civilians had a disability because of conflict, including because of torture and landmine incidents. There were approximately 12,000 amputees in the country--two-thirds believed to be landmine survivors--supported by five physical rehabilitation centers throughout the country, with the Ministry of Home Affairs, in collaboration with ICRC, opening a new center in October in Myitkyina, Kachin State. Persons with disabilities reported stigma, discrimination, and abuse from civilian and government officials. Students with disabilities cited barriers to inclusive education as a significant disadvantage.

Military veterans with disabilities received official benefits on a priority basis, usually a civil service job at equivalent pay, but both military and ethnic-minority survivors in rural areas typically did not have access to livelihood opportunities or affordable medical treatment. Official assistance to nonmilitary persons with disabilities in principle included two-thirds of pay for up to one year for a temporary disability and a tax-free stipend for permanent disability. While the law provides job protection for workers who become disabled, authorities did not implement it.

National/Racial/Ethnic Minorities

Ethnic minorities constitute an estimated 30 to 40 percent of the population, and the seven ethnic-minority states make up approximately 60 percent of the national territory. Wide-ranging governmental and societal discrimination against minorities persisted, including in areas such as education, housing, employment, and access to health services. International observers noted that large wage variations based on religious and ethnic backgrounds were common.

While ethnic-minority groups generally used their own languages at home, Burmese generally remained the mandatory language of instruction in government schools. A February report from the Asia Foundation noted that schools run by ethnic armed groups often operated in the local ethnic language but that even students in well-established local language curricula, such as one operated by the Karen National Union, had limited future options without gaining academic credentials through the national curriculum. In schools controlled by ethnic armed groups, students sometimes had no access to the national curriculum. There were very few domestic publications in indigenous-minority languages.

Tension between the military and ethnic minority populations, while somewhat diminished in areas with ceasefire agreements, remained high, and the army stationed forces in some ethnic groups' areas of influence and controlled certain cities, towns, and highways. Ethnic armed groups, including the Kachin Independence Organization, pointed to the increased presence of army troops as a major source of tension and insecurity. Reported abuses included killings, beatings, torture, forced labor, forced relocations, and rapes of members of ethnic groups by government soldiers. Some groups also committed abuses (see section 1.g.).

Muslims, including the Rohingya in Rakhine State, faced severe discrimination based on their ethnicity and their religion. Interethnic conflict in Rakhine State negatively affected the broader Muslim community, including the primarily Muslim ethnic Kaman. Most Rohingya faced severe restrictions on their ability to travel, avail themselves of health-care services, engage in economic activity (see section 7.d.), obtain an education, and register births, deaths, and marriages (see section 2.d.). The Rohingya population constituted the majority of those displaced by outbreaks of violence across Rakhine State in 2012. Most remained in semipermanent camps with severely limited access to education, health care, and livelihoods.

Acts of Violence, Discrimination, and Other Abuses Based on Sexual Orientation and Gender Identity

Several prominent groups led the charge in promoting support for lesbian, gay, bisexual, transgender, and intersex (LGBTI) persons. Political reforms made it easier for the LGBTI community to hold public events and openly participate in society, yet stigma and a lack of acceptance among the general population persisted. Despite this progress, consensual same-sex sexual activity remains illegal under the penal code, which contains provisions against "sexually abnormal" behavior and entails punishments up to life imprisonment. Laws against "unnatural offenses" apply equally to both men and women. These laws were rarely enforced, but LGBTI persons reported that police used the threat of prosecution to extort bribes. While the penal code is used more for coercion or bribery, the LGBTI community, particularly transgender women, were most frequently charged under paragraph (c) and (d) of the Yangon Police Act 30 (1899)/Police Act 35 (1945), otherwise known as the "shadow and disguise" laws. These laws use the justification that a person dressed or acting in a way that is perceived as not being in line with their biological gender is in "disguise." The LGBTI community also reported broad societal and familial discrimination. According to a report by a local NGO, transgender women reported higher levels of police abuse and discrimination than other members of the LGBTI community.

There were reports of discrimination based on sexual orientation and gender identity in employment. LGBTI persons reported facing discrimination from medical care providers.

HIV and AIDS Social Stigma

The constitution provides for the individual's right to health care in accordance with national health policy, prohibits discrimination by the government on the grounds of "status," and requires equal opportunity in employment and equality before the law. Persons with HIV/AIDS could submit a complaint to the government if a breach of their constitutional rights or denial of access to essential medicines occurred, such as antiretroviral therapy. There were no reports of individuals submitting complaints on these grounds. There are no HIV-specific protective laws or laws that specifically address the human rights aspects of HIV.

There were continued reports of societal violence and discrimination, including employment discrimination, against persons with HIV/AIDS. Negative incidents such as exclusion from social gatherings and activities; verbal insults, harassment, and threats; and physical assaults continued to occur. While laws that criminalize behaviors linked to an increased risk of acquiring HIV/AIDS remain in place, directly fueling stigma and discrimination against persons engaged in these behaviors and impeding their access to HIV prevention, treatment, and care services, advocacy created the most progress in changing attitudes of lawmakers and law enforcement officials. For example, parliament hosted the first-ever HIV/AIDS advocacy session with civil society organizations on World AIDS Day, December 1. Persons with HIV/AIDS could submit a complaint to the Myanmar National Human Rights Commission if violations to their fundamental rights to life or privacy occurred. Nonetheless, the commission's resources and power to resolve individual complaints was limited, and the commission drew significant public criticism for its handling of a child abuse case (see section 5).

Law enforcement practices contributed to high levels of stigma and discrimination against female sex workers that in turn hindered their access to HIV prevention, treatment, and social protection services. Police harassment of sex workers deterred the workers from carrying condoms.

Other Societal Violence or Discrimination

There were a few reports of other cases of societal violence, and anti-Muslim sentiment and discrimination persisted. Members of Bamar-Buddhist nationalist groups, including members of the Buddhist Organization for the Protection of Race and Religion (MaBaTha), continued to denigrate Islam and called for a boycott of Muslim businesses.

Other Muslim complaints included unequal treatment by police, pressures to practice Islam in private, difficulty in obtaining citizenship cards, close monitoring of their travel by local government, and restrictions to education opportunities. In some locations in Rakhine, for example, the local population expressed little distinction between the Kaman and the Rohingya, despite the fact that the Kaman are one of the country's recognized 135 ethnic groups defined by the 1982 constitution. Muslim leaders in West Bago indicated a continuing source of frustration was that most Muslims' ethnic designation on their identity cards is "Indian Bamar," despite no affiliation with India.

In July large crowds destroyed two Muslim places of worship in Lone Khin Village, Kachin State, and Thaye Thamain Village, Waw Township, Bago Division. In both cases contacts alleged that MaBaTha monks led crowds in the attacks, provoked by allegations that the new construction in both cases was illegal. Police arrested a small number of individuals involved in the violence and then released them after five days. The government did not investigate either incident or file charges against any perpetrators by year's end.

Multiple sources noted that restrictions against Muslims and Christians impeded their ability to pursue higher education opportunities and assume high-level government positions and that Muslims were unable to invest and trade freely.

Section 7. Worker Rights

a. Freedom of Association and the Right to Collective Bargaining

The law provides for the right of workers to form and join independent unions, bargain collectively, and conduct legal strikes. The law permits labor organizations to demand the reinstatement of workers dismissed for union activity, but it does not explicitly prohibit antiunion discrimination in the form of demotions or mandatory transfers, or offer protection for workers seeking to form a union. The law does not provide for adequate protections for workers from dismissal before a union is officially registered.

The law permits labor federations and confederations to affiliate with international union federations and confederations. Laws prohibit personnel of the defense services, armed forces, and police force from forming unions. Basic labor organizations must have a minimum of 30 workers and register through township registrars with the Chief Registrar's Office of the Ministry of Labor, Employment, and Social Security (Ministry of Labor). Township labor organizations require at least 10 percent of relevant basic labor organizations to register; regional or state labor organizations require at least 10 percent of relevant township labor organizations. Each of these higher-level unions must include only organizations within the same trade or activity. Similarly, federations and confederations also require a minimum number of regional or state labor organizations (10 percent and 20 percent, respectively) from the next lower level in order to register formally.

The law provides for voluntary registration for local NGOs, including NGOs working on labor issues. Organizations that chose to register could reportedly face more restrictions, including requirements for prior approval from the government if they wished to make changes to organization objectives and activities after registration took place. Broader restrictions on freedom of assembly remained in place (see section 2.b.).

The law gives unions the right to represent workers, to negotiate and bargain collectively with employers, and to send representatives to a conciliation body or conciliation tribunal. The law permits unions to assist in individual disputes and individual employment agreements. The law does not contain detailed measures regarding management of the bargaining process, such as a duty to bargain in good faith, a period for bargaining, registration, or extension or enforcement of collective agreements.

The law provides for the right to strike in most sectors, with a majority vote by workers, permission of the relevant labor federations, and detailed information and three days' advance notice provided to the employer and the relevant conciliation body. The law does not permit strikes or lockouts in essential services. In "public utility services" (including the transport; cargo and freight; postal; sanitation; information, communication, and technology; energy; petroleum; and financial sectors), lockouts are permitted with a minimum of 14 days' notice provided to the relevant labor organizations and conciliation body. Strikes in public utility services require generally the same measures as in other sectors, but with 14 days' advance notice and negotiation between workers and management before the strike takes place to determine maintenance of minimum service levels.

The law provides for a framework for the settlement of individual and collective disputes at the enterprise, township, regional, and national levels through conciliation or arbitration but lacks sufficient mechanisms for enforcement. Ministry of Labor Department of Labor Relations engaged the community on awareness activities surrounding the arbitration process to enforce these mechanisms, despite limited enforcement mechanisms. As part of this process, in December 2015 the Department of Labor Relations published a pamphlet in both English and local languages explaining the conciliation process and the various processes of settling disputes. They also planned to hold seminars for the conciliation body, arbitration body, and arbitration council to include employers, workers, and government representatives in Yangon, Mandalay, and Naypyidaw. Outside observers expressed concern that the process was lengthy and cumbersome and could pose obstacles to workers using it to resolve grievances. The law does not prohibit failure to respect an order of the arbitration council. Penalties for noncompliance with the settlement agreements called for in the law are low: 100,000 kyats ($75) or less than one year in prison. Some observers noted that the low penalty amounts combined with the lack of enforcement enabled some employers to ignore judgments by the arbitration and conciliation body and the provisions of settlement agreements. There were reports of employers appealing council decisions to the Supreme Court. The government reported that 96 percent of industrial disputes between March 2012 and December 2014 took place in Rangoon and that more than 50 percent came from the garment sector.

Labor groups reported their biggest challenge remained labor organizations' inability to register at the national level, a prerequisite for entering labor framework agreements with multinational companies, due to the registration requirements under the law. In addition the ILO, labor activists, and media continued to report concerns that employers subsequently fired or created other forms of reprisal for workers who formed or joined labor unions.

Workers and workers' organizations continued to report that they generally found the Ministry of Labor to be helpful in urging employers to negotiate, but there were consistent reports of employers ignoring the negotiated agreements or engaging in other forms of antiunion discrimination.

Media outlets reported far fewer allegations of dismissal, imprisonment, and beatings of workers for organizing activity than in years past.

On February 29, Myanmar Veneer and Plywood Private Ltd. terminated 128 workers in Sagaing after the workers reportedly demanded overtime pay and better working conditions. This action led to formation of an informal workers association, the Freedom Labor Organization, which organized a march demanding better pay and working conditions. Dozens of workers marched from Sagaing to Naypyidaw starting on April 29. Although police initially allowed the march to take place, as protesters neared the capital on May 18, media reports indicated that 200 police officers dispersed the protest and arrested 71 persons. Authorities released 20 without charge and 36 more on June 1 after dropping the original charges. As of October the remaining 15 persons--10 workers and five student sympathizers--remained in detention pending trial facing a range of charges under the penal code, including unlawful assembly, incitement, and rioting.

b. Prohibition of Forced or Compulsory Labor

Laws prohibit all forms of forced or compulsory labor and provide for the punishment of persons who impose forced labor on others, but the government did not effectively enforce the law.

The law provides for criminal penalties for forced labor violations; penalties differ depending on whether the military, the government, or a private citizen committed the forced labor violation. Prosecution of military perpetrators occurs under either the military or penal code. Civilian perpetrators may be subject to administrative action or criminal proceedings under the penal code. The maximum penalty under the penal code is 12 months in prison; under the military code it is seven years in prison. International observers deemed the penalties sufficient to deter forced labor.

The government continued to implement the ILO action plan to eliminate forced labor even following its expiration in March, renewing this mechanism in November with the ILO. Both the military and the government responded to complaints logged by the complaints mechanism on an ad hoc basis during the lapse in the ILO mechanism. The ILO reported that it continued to receive reports indicating that the use of forced labor was decreasing overall, but the number of complaints of forced labor through the ILO complaints mechanism remained significant. Moreover, it noted that the government's and military's use of forced or compulsory labor of adults and children and the failure to hold perpetrators accountable remained a problem (see section 7.c.). As of September the ILO received an average of 25 complaints monthly, compared with 33 complaints monthly in 2014. The ILO attributed the continuing high rates of reporting to increasing awareness of the illegality of forced labor along with strong support networks provided by the ILO and civil society organizations and the continued low levels of public trust and confidence in the national justice system. The government completed a new negotiated framework with the ILO in November.

Reports of forced labor occurred across the country, including in cease-fire states, and the prevalence was higher in states with significant armed conflict. Forced labor continued, including forced portering, mandatory work on public infrastructure projects, and activities related to the military's "self-reliance" policy. Under the self-reliance policy, military battalions are responsible for procuring their own food and labor supplies from local villagers--a major contributing factor to forced labor and other abuses. Some observers noted that forced labor practices were changing, resulting in a reported decrease in use of forced labor by the military and an increase in reports of forced labor in the private sector and by civilian officials. At the same time, international organizations reported that forced labor remained common in areas affected by conflicts.

The ILO received reports of forced labor in the private sector, including excessive overtime with or without compensation by workers at risk of losing their job and bonded labor. Domestic workers also remained at risk of domestic servitude. Forced labor on palm oil and rubber plantations or in jade and precious stone mines occurred. There were reports of forced child labor (see section 7.c.).

Also see the Department of State's *Trafficking in Persons Report* at
www.state.gov/j/tip/rls/tiprpt/.

c. Prohibition of Child Labor and Minimum Age for Employment

In January the government amended the 1951 Shops and Establishments Act and
the 1951 Factories Act, banning the employment of children under the age of 14
and including special provisions for "youth employment" above 14. For instance,
employees between the ages of 14 and 16 can work only in a "nonhazardous
environment" and can work only up to four hours per day. Employees ages 16-18
must have a certificate to authorize them to carry out "work fit for an adult." The
law prohibits employees under 18 from working in a hazardous environment.

Trained inspectors monitored the application of these new regulations, including
with regard to child labor, but a general lack of resources hindered inspectors
deployed throughout the country. Inspectors from the Ministry of Social Welfare
monitored child related cases at 25 Township Community on the Rights of the
Child projects throughout the country. The Ministry of Labor worked with
UNICEF on problems related to child protection and minimum age and worked
with the ILO to address child labor. In 2014 the Ministry of Labor, with ILO
support, established a child labor working group, chaired by the minister and
composed of representatives from all government departments, the private sector,
labor unions, and civil society. The government tasked a working group with
drafting a national plan of action to implement ILO Convention 182 on the
Elimination of the Worst Forms of Child Labor. On August 29, the government
presented the findings of its 2015 Labor Force Survey, including statistics on child
labor. In September the minister of labor, immigration, and population submitted a
draft list of hazardous occupations for children to the National Tripartite Dialogue
Forum for review, following its approval by a technical working group composed
of multiple ministries.

The law provides criminal penalties for those found guilty of recruiting child
soldiers, and the government continued making progress towards eliminating
recruitment in the military of children (also see section 1.g.). The criminal
penalties for military officials under martial law range from dismissal from service
and imprisonment in civil prison to a fine of seven days' pay. For civilians the
Trafficking in Persons law outlines penalties for child recruitment from a minimum
of 10 years to a maximum of life imprisonment. Penalties under the law and their
enforcement for other child labor violations were insufficient to deter violations.

Child labor remained prevalent and highly visible. Children were at high risk, since poor economic conditions induced destitute parents to remove them from school after, and occasionally before, they completed compulsory education. In cities children worked mostly in the food-processing and light-manufacturing industries, as street vendors or refuse collectors, as restaurant and teashop attendants, and as domestic workers.

The Ministry of Labor worked with other ministries to collect better data on existing child labor and started a campaign directed at parents to raise awareness of the risks of child labor and provide information about other education options available to children. The ILO recently published its report on the demographics surrounding awareness of child labor in three areas of the country (Rangoon, the Ayeyarwady region, and Mon State). The Ministry of Labor used this information to create a more targeted awareness campaign and engaged with the Ministry of Education on two programs, one aimed at bringing children out of the workplace and putting them in school, and another to support former child soldiers in pursuit of classroom education or vocational training. As part of the new government's "100 day plan," the Labor Ministry launched vocational schools to train young workers for jobs in nonhazardous environments. The government coordinated its efforts with the ILO in an effort to benefit directly 3,600 children and 1,000 households with education, worker safety, and support services in the Mon, Ayeyarwady, and Rangoon target areas.

With few or no skills, increasing numbers of children worked in the informal economy or in the street, exposing them to drugs and petty crime, risk of arrest, commercial sexual exploitation, and HIV/AIDS and other sexually transmitted diseases (also see section 6, Children).

Children were vulnerable to forced labor in teashops, agriculture, and begging. In rural areas children routinely worked in family agricultural activities, occasionally in situations of forced labor.

While the government liberated child soldiers and reported disciplining military officials for recruiting them in some cases, reports indicated that members of the military continued to recruit and use children in military-related activities. Ethnic armed groups reportedly also continued to recruit child soldiers (see section 1.g.).

d. Discrimination with Respect to Employment and Occupation

Labor laws and regulations do not specifically prohibit employment discrimination based on race, color, sex, religion, gender, political opinion, national origin or citizenship, social origin, disability, sexual orientation or gender identity, age, language, HIV-positive status or other communicable diseases, or social status.

There were reports government and private actors practiced anti-Muslim discrimination that impeded Muslim-owned businesses' operations and negatively affected their ability to hire and retain labor, maintain proper working standards, and secure public and private contracts. There were reports of discrimination based on sexual orientation and gender identity in employment, including the denial of promotions and firing of LGBTI persons. Activists reported that job opportunities for many openly gay and lesbian persons were limited, and they noted a general lack of support from society as a whole. Activists reported that in addition to general societal discrimination, persons with HIV/AIDS faced employment discrimination in both the public and private sector, including suspensions and the loss of employment following positive results from mandatory workplace HIV testing.

e. Acceptable Conditions of Work

In September 2015 the government adopted an official minimum daily wage of 3,600 kyats ($2.70). The minimum wage covers a standard eight-hour workday across all sectors and industries and applies to all workers except for those in businesses with fewer than 15 employees. The announcement did not include any mention of overtime compensation, which, as was the case for the minimum wage, had been a contentious issue of debate over the previous two years between the government, employers, and workers. The National Tripartite Dialogue Forum was working through such questions, especially regarding overtime pay, through the end of the year. Estimates placed the national poverty income level at less than 1,000 kyats ($.75) per day.

On January 25, parliament passed the Payment of Wages Act. This law updates the 1936 law and requires employers to pay employees on the date the salary is due for companies with 100 employees or less. For companies with more than 100 employees, the employer is required to pay employees within five days from the designated payday. Also in January the government amended the 1951 Factories Act and the 1951 Shops and Establishments Act to mandate that overtime cannot exceed 12 hours per workweek and can exceed 16 hours in a workweek only on special occasions. The amendments also stipulate that an employee's total working hours cannot exceed 11 hours per day (including overtime and a one-hour break) and applies to shops, commercial establishments, and establishments for public entertainment.

Recent legislation relating to occupational safety and health enacted in during the year included the Laws Relating to the Environment, Safety in the Use of Chemicals and Hazardous Substances, Boiler Act, and Electricity Act. The Labor Dispute Law stipulates the terms and conditions required for occupational safety, health, welfare, and productivity, but information is limited as to whether a worker can remove themselves from situations that endanger their health or safety without jeopardizing their employment.

The Ministry of Labor's Factories and General Labor Laws Inspection Department oversees labor conditions in the private sector. Both resources and capacity constrained enforcement. In 2014 the ministry had 99 general labor law inspectors, 104 occupational safety and health inspectors, and 53 inspection offices for the country. While the inspectors had the technical knowledge, they did not have the equipment necessary to execute inspections properly. In certain sectors other ministries regulated occupational safety and health laws, for example the Ministries of Agriculture and Irrigation, Industries, Mines, and Health.

The law stipulates that disputes in special economic zones be settled in accordance with original contracts and existing laws. Under the 2013 Myanmar Special Economic Zone Law, the government appointed a labor inspector for each such zone and established zonal tripartite committees responsible for setting wage levels and monitoring the ratio of local and foreign labor.

On September 28-30, the government and ILO held the country's second labor stakeholders forum under the auspices of the multipartner Initiative to Promote Fundamental Labor Rights and Practices in Myanmar. The forum brought together more than 200 participants from the public and private sectors to discuss labor rights and various labor problems, including addressing child labor, strengthening labor dispute settlement, and strengthening local capacity and institutions.

Enforcement of the laws generally took place in the government sector, but frequent violations occurred in private enterprises. The Union Parliament Joint Commission did not resume its work reviewing labor violations. Workers continued to submit complaints to relevant government agencies and the dispute settlement mechanism. Workers' organizations alleged that government inspections were rare and often announced with several days' notice that allowed factory owners to bring facilities--often temporarily--into compliance. Corruption and bribery of inspectors reportedly occurred.

The social security board covers all employees in companies with more than five employees, with the exception of six sectors (government, international organizations, seasonal farming and fisheries, construction, nonprofit organizations, and domestic work). In practical terms the board covered primarily industrial zones, the location of the majority of registered workers, and therefore supported less than 1 percent of individuals involved in workplace accidents or casualties. While the board provided hospitals and clinics, it did not keep independently verifiable statistics on accidents or workplace violations. Observers assumed workers in other sectors of the economy to have even less support, and no statistics on accidents or workplace violations were available.